LEA

VING

CLE

POEMS OF NOMADIC DISPERSAL

JANICE A. LOWE

MIAMI UNIVERSITY PRESS

Library of Congress Cataloging-in-Publication Data

Names: Lowe, Janice A.

Title: Leaving CLE : poems of nomadic dispersal / by Janice A. Lowe.

Other titles: Poems of nomadic dispersal

Description: Oxford, Ohio : Miami University Press, 2016.

Identifiers: LCCN 2015043178 | ISBN 9781881163596 (pbk.)

Classification: LCC PS3612.O883 A6 2016 | DDC 811/.6—dc23

LC record available at http://lccn.loc.gov/2015043178

Cover collage: Julie Patton, *ju leaf shoes*

Design by Quemadura

Printed on acid-free, recycled paper

in the United States of America

Miami University Press

356 Bachelor Hall

Miami University

Oxford, Ohio 45056

FOR *MOM*, WILLA GREEN LOWE, WHO REVELS IN THE SOULS OF WORDS

IN CELEBRATORY MEMORY OF *WALTER J. LOWE*,
THE BIG BROTHER WHO GIFTED ME LPS AND 45S

AND DAD, *W. JAMES LOWE* FOR INFUSING ACTIVISM WITH LOVE,
FOR STRETCHING TIME

SNOW WILL NOT KEEP A PAIR OF HANDCUFFS *RUSSELL ATKINS*

CREPUSCULAR PORTRAITS

CORPOREAL MIGRATION

INTRODUCTION

These poems are born from memory and chase a mutable idea of hometown. They catch up with past furies. They play dodgeball with the half-forgotten, with moments recalled in minute detail and with a historical, musical Cleveland. Although I've exchanged hometowns and regions many times—5 with my family and 5 on my own—many of the poems refer to the 1970s, when my close-knit family lived in Cleveland for a second time. We returned to Cleveland from the East Coast during the euphoric re-election campaign of Carl B. Stokes, the city's first black mayor. I grew up with a politically active, community-minded father and his colleagues who rubbed shoulders with elected officials and demanded that they work in the holistic interest of neighborhoods. Dad taught me to love Cleveland, The People. Mom immersed us in the arts there. I never looked at Cleveland as *the mistake on the lake*. I was too busy enjoying the cultural and civic hubbub.

When I was in high school, my family moved to Tuscaloosa, Alabama, the home territory of the father I adored. That shift created a flashbulb memory of events around the move, of my clumsy navigation of a new cultural scape and chronic longing to live the story I'd constructed of what my late teen years would have been.

ELECTROMAGNETIC SIDEWALKS

BROOKLYN

RESISTANCE GIRL T

what's in the tea bag, Mami?

              sumtin natural
              roots 'n bliss out

                                    a soothing pick-me-up
                                      talking leaves

fired up sleepwalker's protection
a main-----------------tain

             what's in the **tea**, Mami?

              who u taught collecting
              harvest
              read up
              try it out on

                                    twig and twig after
                                    twig

proper-----ties?

why u not property?   who taught u   owning?

what's the T, Mami?

tell us something aromatic
sell us some loose sense-u-all
some lose your mind

hair in dere

a loc   I wouldn't drink   should I?

she would or he   cuz you—it smells so good

what's in the bag Mami?
can u cure   tinnitus?
chemo ragged taste buds?
cure
pedestrian rage
cure
spring sneezing
too much too public transportation

u know when u can't stand no more
being a human sandwich in the morning?

not free as a platform rat

is your name Super Moon ImmuniTee-ee-ee-ee÷?

Mami I'll take all the ounces
I can get

for this

RESTORATION (A SONG)

Re   store   race   shun
    re   Store   Race   shun

Restore books   restore store   re Store Asian   Restore Black blocks
    restore Lady   Restore Asian

Asian Black Power Woman Lady Runaway Green West Indian Korean Market Refugeeeeeeeeee

Clocking locking eyes
Hear a soulcroon in her best Badu,

                         "You people think you're white!"

About to call me out
going in on me

                         "Cold Brew Coffee Negro"

                        You ou ou ou ou ou ou **yo**u ou ou ou ou ou

Me??

                  -ou ou ou ou ou ou ou ou
                  "Think you're **white**"

Black Power Lady Who Happens to Be **A**sian   **Black** Power
Black **P**ower Lady Who Happens to Be **A**sian   **Asian**

Funky Janelle **M**onae precision
Misty Twirling **C**opeland by the Patty Shop

Re   sto   ration   is good twice
a secret nod   sly smiles

The "that's what's up"
the "**good** good"

the corner, "Hey"

sunshine rainy new-ews
the lend-you-a-hands

Black Power Woman Who Happens to be Asian
Black Power Woman Who happens to be Asian
would play you some **Jean Grae**

Luv my MCs

Would give you a ten-spot if you say you're broke
even if you don't respect her kimchee

Asian Black Power Lady is sick of cash talking

brownstones walking

A Santigold wil'ing out she tears up those signs

those **We Buy Houses Cash sigh-igh-signs**

Tell it like Talib

Take you to the pan yard

She'll take you to the pan yard
steelband pan yard

for socas and more

She wants to save restore and more
bedroom blocks and gardens
while you can still get ya afro locs or short blonde 'do tight
for something un-be-weave-able

                                    reasonable

                                    Plum tea herbals miso squeezed juice

                                    black soap shea butter island soul fillet

Unsolicited "hellos" advice

elegantly worded street compliments

She knows Jacob Lawrence's corner

Nostrand and Fulton is her pocket   *Loop that*

Nostrand and Fulton is her pocket

                                    *Do it, **Shirley***

*Unbossed like **Chisholm***

AH~~~~~~

~~~~~~

~~~~~~

Retweet this   *Grace Lee Boggs*   *Retweet this*   *Kochiyama*

Retweet this   *Ichioka*   *Retweet this*   *Retweet this*

BPWWHTBA

If you want to find the fakeass reggae and ska party you gotta get through me.

Speak the right code I might let you in. Do not ask about The Notorious B.I.G. tours or

what Billy Joel was singing about that scared speculators but if you mention the mural

you know Ol' Dirty Bastard on a benefit card you might be golden.

Re   store   race   shun

           Re   store   race   shun

EDGE-A-CATION

New York C**ity-ity**

                     Whooo New **York** C*ity-ity*   **New York** C**ity-ity**

      Whooop New **York** C*ity-ity*

                                          THE   ***BK***

                                          WHOOOOO   *the **bk***

                                         HA   ***The BK***

Nieuw Breukelen

an artist uncooperative knitting space

a café/laundry drop off/artist wake up service

the one bilking u for a $200/month espresso fix when what you need is

space

something other than a wall   vitamin d   viable savings accountability

saving from screens   soluble protein   indivisible neighbors of color

***strive** Striver*

portfolio poor and brownstone rich is the new various

talk to the realtor on her foghorn celly

convince her that all of Park Slope is closer to Brooklyn Bridge

than Pratt Institute (wink wink)

*do **n**ot share your borrowed tabloid/Times with an artisanal water hawker*

*d**o** bogart the community table from Jogging Dude refusing to rest his heart rate long*

enough to clean up after overworked sweat glands dripping on you

small batches of

intolerance   ok ok, NOT Ok

*d***on't do that   encourage**

a nuanced local edge

edge   *ah-iight* **along with yogic**

flexibility

I   LOVE   THE   EDGE (sing it 2x)

*I   LOVE   THE   **EDGE***

biked here   *bonus*

born here   *you work too hard to cede your corner of industrial islands to stirred hips*

New York **C**ity-**ity**

Whooo New **York C**ity-**ity**   **New York C**ity-**ity**

Whooop New **York C**ity-**ity**

THE BK

WHOOOOO   *the*

bk   HA   ***The***

BK

SIGN

1.

My   boy
friend once   **Sign of**
he   'so   n   me
He don't   k   now   when
to
stop Pounding   i   n   me

URBAN

                                        May
                                        be   she's the baby
                              Sit   t   er   no   t t   he moth   er
Typical 3rd world ignorance
                                        Typical 1st wo   rld arrogance
Trya response typical of your stereo
Type   Start   **de KKK**
by learning to spell
                                        You mis   read the spell
                                        i   n   g
Bergen St.
Why don't you take some of your 3rd world arro   **F Train**
gance and teach the 3rd wor   ld

2.

Why get all thin-skinned about racist subway chicken scratch?
Is comeback graffiti good practice or wasted rhyme?

Sarcasm like strength overrates
Muscles comes in handy for doing-it-yourself space saving renovations
Emotional machismo kicks in when a situation calls
Only the breezy survive courage
What you need is more bounce
a cap juggling flip flying pole defying rock steadying uptown "A" trancer
pole dangling upside down in blue-gold paisley pj bottoms

his head's got it

      more bounce

Lords of Train
getting crunk in a crawl space
Eyefuls of afrobatic beat
giving your ears *the most* in underground philosophy:

      a. Hip Hop is Reiki

      b. An endorphin-inducing rush hour is a cosmic giggle

      c. The art you run from could save someone from pretension, maybe you

Pay the passed hat/ignore it/accept the rush

The Nimble roll around in choices

I filch Nimble Feet's stage whisper:

"Don't Say Thank You. That makes our shit dumb."

LETTER OPENER

it's fasting time
days name the missing
tips massage the neighborhood cute consignment shop
you sip patois   the counter guy crooning   want to cast
him in a play   you don't know your budget or that his
name is Victor   Victor known for karaoke but wanting to
get into theater   post blizzard Victor's girlfriend comes
to warm him   this lucky dude s(l)ings *Customer Care*
live enough to shake a store front conjures a dancehall
twist of compressed and regular bargain seekers   real
life doesn't yet know of your four day fast   your just for
a minute consideration of his insides   him   driving a
humongous rig on 20 days of empty   you absent from
his beard's caresses

is no small price to pay
for piety

softest parts of him may
slow your roll

coax you to mi ni mal

MIGRATORY REVERSAL

Best Location in the Nation

O-H-I-O

they call Alabama The Crimson Tide

OH-H-EYE-OWE

BONE HUGS BEST LOCATION BLUES

woe mack woe mack   woe mack woe mack

get up   wake up   can't stay (a)sleep

cuz call me Chuck
hole up in the cut
living lake effect grind
ditch topical rewind
when I fl- fl- flow

You the beach   wave wave
*   cle town gravel   rain over*
I'm the beach   wave wave
*   cle town gravel   wash over   watch over*
rain
*   wash over   watch over   wash over*

Good stuff about Cleveland
good---lots of it
decades of anti Bob Hopes and Arsenio Halls
become laugh track writers anonymous
instigate late night Forest City bashing all the way to the bank

CLE rock hauls and take a joke
            and we can talk some trash if you got some cash
            blows Bull Moose

How many Frankie Yankovics and Bull Moose Jacksons
does it take to save a public utility?

Run it down like Jim Brown

How many abandoned boogie woogie accordions
re-purpose themselves as bridges?

Count mobsters needed to take out **The Boy Mayor**
his refusal to sell Muni Light set up some **Shock Theater**
not the **Ghoulardi** I don't remember and his late-night horror movie hosting frolics
or **The Ghoul's** giddily obvious homage but real blood draining shock

Drum roll   a hit man
a one-a and a two-a in the Kucinich
Columb**us N**ightmare **D**ay   **This movie's so bad**
Parade of serendipity   **phone knock** landing Mayor Dennis in the hospital
for um "unrelated reasons"   **Kucinich**
Noggin unavailable for target   leaving him to liberalize despite conservatives

in his return to public eyelife

Cleveland rusts Cleveland's trust
the city's rock and hard ass place banking on The People to default
leaning hard on The People post Muni Light's pay up mandate
better to **Call** and **Post**

How many
        Kucinichs foil a pay to play?
        spitballs does Gaylord Perry sneak pitch?
        Russell Means are mistaken for Chief Wahoo?
        Dawg Pounds morph into Ravens Roosts?

How much sulfur is required for Smell-o-vision?
Is a steel mill better imagined?

Is St. Theodosius Cathedral
church by day
progressive club crawl end spot
til earliest

light?
Skinny filaments of gold light outline
hovering clouds of pre-grunge Fagan's
a decked out sky ready for a weekend in The Flats
jazzily punk daybreak
soulblues polka varietal sun plunge
hoppish hippish gospel in the AM reveal
Ohio Players   Zapp featuring Roger   Bootsy   Isley Bros.
funkin all ways back 2 you through your nitelight
The Agora a dream you read about in **Scene** but vanished from before you could catch
Devo in Cleve OH

Now Little Jimmy Scott and Junie Morrison
could snake charm rivers from Dayton on down or up
the Cuyahoga included
                            Sing it Junie:
                            listen to the water side of you
A striped city
so stylish
Black East White West
swirl in between
Hungarian Chinese Lebanese Puerto Rican pockets Polish
Jewish sleeves   a Little Cuba marrying White or Black
became Polish or Black Southern or Italian inflected Cubanos

infamy of Big Italy eclipsed by Murray Hill's

Italian specialties   curio shops and tomato gardens

Fig preservation societies

Have your bed and breakfast quaint now and all historically marked

where you used to ride your bike and get chased out or worse

now that North Coast is pure unadulterated unlegislated progress?

Don't look into a Buckeye's eyes unless you mean Love—Rust Belt Style

How many times can I abandon the East Side?

How cavernously can I

Love a city

that gave me Girl Scout meetings at The Sir Rah Jazz/Disco Club

sparkly stuff spicing up our merit badge and cookie business

conducted in Spanish by a retired high school teacher

determined to field trip us to Madrid

THE KARAMU OF DEER ON THE BUS

They got the memo
"Deer taking the bus," says Arcey
"Animals coming back into The City"
Taking chances on "C" streets
Carnegie, Chester, St. Clair, Central

Called by clarinets of Severance
Or maybe
Barking Spider gauzy blue jams

Raccoons did this
Calling deer to roam when school let out
For mixing into the palette
Of Cleveland's black brown and tan school kid universe

Sensing precariousness
Ohio's open carry out in the county-ness
Deer avoid Wal-Mart
And the occasional city dweller bored w/gun
Trying out a territorial venison change from human beef

Bambi and co. scatter
Urban gardens
Matchbook lawns
City swaths of national green

A novel swim in the Lake
Antlers poking through ocean lake blue
Getting a look at a lighthouse
The understory

Finn remembers
While visiting his poet dad in CLE
Chasing chipmunks you know like Alvin

Certainly no deer
Trotted my neighborhood
Back in the days
Maybe you'd see a rabbit or 3
In the flower bed

Maybe one has to get next to downtown
To feel it
The "C" of the city
Eclectic CLE
~~Higbee's~~ Hype a casino now if you go in for that sort of thing
Hurry of ~~Halle's~~   office space now
Play of the House
Tall of Terminal
Refurbished cherished old
Or tasteful new construction
Clouds gazing tips of Towers
Ghosted replays of Cleveland's Broadway
Val's in the Alley
Jimmy Owens and his after hours spot
Keeping horn players in beers long into blaring morning
After Doan's Corners swept up its last bar stool huggers
You heard future **Eye Ay Ayler** 105 times swinging that bell
Albert Eyes summoning day

Jostle and hustle and mayhem of
Street Corner
Red whiskered brown preacher

In front of ~~May Co~~. (apartments) crossing streets with
The hurried
Pointing at the unsuspecting or the used-to-it
"You're Going to Hell" *openly carrying on*
Packing hellified heat
What would the ever-direct Rev. Street Corner say?
"You're going the way of Euclid Ave."
Gone grandeur gone
Black-owned   dry cleaners to hotels

Outta here like a Larry Doby home run at Municipal
Online theme park of CLE past

What would the ever direct
Rev. Street Corner have to say
About that?

Would he have time
After proselytizing Underground CLE
To holler at the Arcade?

a time ago on his New York job
Dad took lunch with the custodial staff
Was told, "You can't do that. We
don't do that here."
His reply, "I don't know about you. I eat lunch with my friends."

5 days a week in CLE, Dad would sharpen Civil Service pencils
Drink coffee   visit the water cooler
Re-read the pre-amble to the Constitution
Etched big in marble in a Federal Bldg. foyer
refused to train young white new hires

For promotion above him but would joke chat drink coffee visit water cooler etc.
For one solid year in protest
"You're not going to train us, are you, Mr.?"

Dad carried an open coolness
*Would say, in his best **WJMO** voice, "You are not the problem"*

The family fondness for Street Corner was a thing
We heard about him often
Shocking the under-initiated

Scaring tourists
While looking like an almost kindly blood
Uncle

THE END OF CHICAGO

"You're overqualified." He was leaving a job interview downtown one day and spotted a bundle on the sidewalk. $500, it turned out to be. Was dry cold out—no snow on the ground. He looked around, put his foot on the wad, picked it up, put it under his coat, walked fast as he could to the nearest "L." The next day, he and the wife moved, exchanged Midwest for East.

JAM AVENUE, QUEENS

red-orangey light
Sinclair Dinosaur pokes his head and neck through a window
glass shatters
wakes the little kids
the cousins
toys of cousins
jolts Union Hall St. and South Rd.
temporarily immobilizes bigger brothers and sisters playing sunset handball
halts the *get down* to Cold Sweat in the foyer
delays laundromat trips
and the ice cream man

a Jamaica Avenue store window
bursts of magenta flowers and peace signs decorate canned air
mod mini and geometrically compelling sandals beckon
the music of lilting dialects

the neighbors are pentecostal praise songs
beauty shops with lots of mirrors
vats of cheery colored hair rollers
Black Panthers alerting on everything

Mother feels crowded by the temporary
wonders if our cousins' welcome of us has expired
Library schools us until a move is agreed on
A couple reconsiders Newark

Mrs. Perry's boarding house

was years before my younger brother and I were born

Mother would type her grad lit papers there, into the night

determined she'd never again call around to ask,

"Do you hire Negroes?"

SANCTIFIED BLASTING
BODDIE RECORDING CO.

If it's mechanical, Mr. Boddie can fix it better than new

He's known for recording everybody in the city

Crystal Illusions, The Headlines, the family band on your block

Enter for the Lord

Exit with a tape

Fix your stereo, television set—organs, cars anything

A Luau of fixing in Cleveland

That '49 Chevrolet I had in college, the one that drove only backwards

The one the Huntsville, AL police warned me to quit driving

"Don't bring that wreck back down The Hill, Boy"

Boddie coulda fixed my broke down ride in two seconds

The brother actually makes vinyl

He's back there in the garage cooking up oil, acetate plates and pouring LPs

You don't remember the embargo?

Oil companies would freeze out Black record companies until White guys got theirs

Ol' Boddie would grind up the cast off records

You hear me   he made new vinyl out of the old

That brother's gonna help us get Stokes re-elected

And record that ballad you wrote for your sweetheart

You wanna sing?

He will record and press you into a 45 rpm bad notes and all

You can bless the neighborhood with it like you're a professional

press your love on one side
colored costs a few cents more

I'm thinking of asking Boddie to drive in the Mount Pleasant Community Association Parade
Get the message out about all the candidates
No float, no teenage Union Avenue Street Club queen
But Boddie Recording Co. for Stokes loudspeakers
Doing their what-you-know-good best through the car roof
RE-ELECT **CARL B. STOKES** for black vinyl

a groove you can't remove

MAYOR OF CLEVELAND

black the color of vinyl
colored cost a few cents more
profess a love on A side
B might push you out the

door

BOY FLOWER

TAMIR

Boy
ritual
streamed
in digital
pixelated
bits
sacrificial bytes
mother father sister
no memory enough
a shaming
a *taming*
a killing

Wannabe Headline

Rogue
humanists
offer alternate
ways to look at
black boys
a different kind of imaging
anything else

Headlines

Father rap *sheeeeit*!

Mother presses conference

Sister Wrestled to Ground

whip

      lash

lash

      back

Tamir grew ?

Question mark wants to know *when*

around violence

Flower Boy in the View Finder

boy flower by-the-lake

his violet weediness

the chlorophyll of him

park innards

A growing green

heirloom boy

heritage seedling of the Western Reserve

Boy

air softing

`````````~~~~~racing grass

growing shy

or mouthy

growing out of shoes

ellipsis

## In View

land banks

urban preserves

## tree planting

## parties

## Family Swim

monitored

vacant edges

Other exciting activities

## Fitness
## watershed

## In the Viewfinder

An "isn't he cute" a lion cub

club

privileged hunter

play gamer

A shaky cop

## LUNCH

::::::::::::::

::::::::::::::

## Search

## Cudell Rec in summer

Sundeck        Sauna

Game room      gym

## BASEBALL
## A*q*u*a*c*i*s*e

Water gains weight

If you enjoy the outdoors

Permission slips
`````````

SCHEDULE

"and pointing it at people.
Probably a juvenile, you
know? . . . I don't know if it's
real or not, you know?"

911 caller said he's
scaring the expletive out of
inaudible

police
car stops
at 0:19 by
0:21 the boy

is ground

Claim Rice failed to put his
hands   up

Hospital rush

day child mortally wounded

Sunday expired
The boy Tamir

Edge of water
gone

Think July and

firepower

working

too damned well

a time ago
Euclid Beach

Aero Dips

Racing Coaster

Flying Turns

The Thriller

Question Mark

they are lovely   did Rice grow up around violets

violins   Severance Hall   the orchestra

he was a **V** not for victory but velocity

question mark

cultural garden called weediness

period

wildfast

Natural History
identifies 136 tree
and plant species; 46
species of sedges,
grasses, mosses,
ferns and fungi; 56
**bird species; seven
amphibian and
reptile species; six
mammal species;
and 89 insect and
arthropod species**

violets

in the midwest are removed

or sprayed

or transplanted from native
beds to edges

will eventually cover lawns and
create a monoculture

remove wild strawberries
from traffic areas because
they tend to die and leave

muddy patches

Re: violets and strawberries
Have you found that they get too pushy
over time and shouldn't be encouraged?

purple violets growing in mostly full sun   white violets in
partial shade

in the mosaic of grasses
they can handle some mowing and foot traffic

I don't see any reason that you can't encourage them

exotic species
watch out

Nov. 26th article

history

justification

domestic

question mark

violins

mother *and* father

Cudell Corns Park
streamline
keep your readers hooked

Write a Review

Upload a photo

A recording
violins

Only in Cleveland

He was living in a gang
infested neighborhood
confirms he was a gangster

Cleveland Hopes

*Who shoots a
12-year-old from 10
feet away and expects
a free pass?*

Violet dreams

modesty

fortune

death too soon

soon too

Color Theory purple
confidence

Ballistic Eyes   power intuition

hitting each other with non-mental spheres

Floriograph   intuition

The orange tip   candor

how to distinguish airsoft guns from real firearms

innocence   if white shows

Euclid Beach Park Riot

protests 1946

"no sitting, no talking, no mixing of any kind . . . between the

races"

Congress of Racial Equality (CORE) put out by park police

Lynn Coleman and Henry MacKey intervene

They are Black cops   off-duty

Fight

Coleman was shot

with his own gun

(see below)

Cleveland Hopes

See below

An officer shot a kid

That is the issue

YEARS CORNER

My world war II post bungalow white
black-trimmed picture window house
rose today
My tiger lilies yellows
John's solitary apple growing tree   plus
huge old evergreens shadowed the side
the walk we couldn't cross
George & us
we ran around fenced grown-ups   red
poison berries barbecue house   sweet
grass & dandelion milk
Hide-seeking George
crosses deaf into a Lincoln   My
continental George we forgot
that walk   My shadowed evergreen
mom salted sandy slid to her back
ice stayed through winter
stubborn as burning lake slippery
like Leroy Kelly on a bullet

MY HOUSE IN CLEVELAND
ELM TREE, THE DENIAL
REVENGE & DAD'S PROPOSAL

my House was small her secrets
full of wild flower memory of Hungarian
table wines her backyard of mint
and rose breath singing through
humble cracks a milk chute
for bottles no longer delivered
her garage a sentry box
weary from Black sightings the
inevitable advance of Color

I denied her size
even as I loved my attic solo room
even as I missed my grown siblings
Walt   Tranita   Bob
it felt like a 2-kid family

would bike
Glendale to 177th to Scottsdale
across suburb v. city barricades
riding almost to mansions up
and leaving dainty urban colonials
white tiny bungalows
2-bedroom squeezed

families in selective memory
for pool houses grander kitchens
of prepper buddies
grander than Sentry guarding
retreated Italians

as Back Porch grooved
to "Wanted Young Man Single and Free"
boat cars chit chat shoulder to shoulder
mid-street, the block at their funky mercy
& l'il kids tradin steps with elders
watchin

House wanted to know
why I didn't get dropped off
at the playground on Wendy
play it off by riding down Harvard to our street
tho Elm Tree could see almost to Jo Ann Dr.

a blown light bulb tripped me up attic stairs
back of hands scrape hard walls
sea green paint like swirled frozen icing
low ceilings catching my sweat
working my stumbling to the half bath faucet for rinsing
water rusty yellow sweet
i drank penance what more could she do

Dad said we'd have room
Down South
Football field for John
Tennis court for daughter
a pool for "The Protester" and "Bright Eyes"
House sent me away

CLE'S J-5

is a singing group a group if nobody hears?
is disembodied emotion the bridge?
manager verse
neighbor verse
investor chorus
school boy hook
an O'Jay's assistance
outro

A five-point star
2 sets of twins
and a singleton

the crowd

2+2+1

slaps tile

Ponderosa Twins plus One
they doing their whole act in the kitchen
c'mon
pulling ceiling down to knees
twirling linoleum
shaking loose wrinkles of preteen love
shimmy knees spin slide
knee drops low lean
knee back jumps front
knee hands glide

arms dislocate

air honestly

splits

the cover *YOU SEND ME*

more propulsion than simmer

more raw than Cooke

what better business for a bail bondsman?

not too many can produce

a Cleveland J-5

Mr. See Brown manages teenyboppin' worksong

must be some kind of luck in here

some tapping the four corners of a grand plan

naming the radio after royalties

that's them, I've got the 45

or listening all night to WJMO

for 2+2+1 singing *Bound,* Ponderosa Style

kill killing it killed   *BOU-ound*

                                        BOUND

                            BOU-ound

                                            BOUND

                    Bound to Fall-all in Love

splash that har-mo-ny

out here we don't live close

to the river but imagine it clean

this edge of the city isn't by the lake

but we feel it clean

out here our street clubs

make sure our ground is *clean* clean

yes cle was major
the Stokes brothers and their Black firsts
mayoral Carl and congressional Louis
don't sing but their Buffalo cousin
Rick James is a punkfunk wonder
they pump this idea about
making the river a river again
shooooooooooooooooosshh

non-flammable potable
cruise to anywhere worthy Detroit ferry sound
example for the country of what Black hatching
clean water act of do it now
can do

we weren't always out this way
we lived in a house I grew out of knowing
a 2-family painted yellow like buttercups growing in a road
mom & dad took us by to see the neighbors
I picture the family there
the time I dropped the clothes no one knew I could reach
all of them out of the window
an entertainment of air surfing pastels

17 years older to the day
my brother carried me everywhere
took me proudly for royal blue Chevy rides
until the girls asked him, "Is that *your* baby?"
I know he held me close
singing Stax and Motown under breath
swaying on 1 2 3 & 4

I got the best hand-me-downs

Sly   The Meters   Isaac Hayes   Lee Morgan   Martha Reeves and The Vandellas   The Isley Brothers

bet he had some Boddie records too

somewhere

gotta look for them

SOME YEARS DAD WAS PRESIDENT

Who is the man who wants to save Cleveland from chuckholes?

Who is the man who pied-pipered block parties as community clean-ups?

Who is the man who ingested astrology and Robert's Rules of Order as vitamins for community debate facilitation?

Who is the vet who taught Sunday School so the little kids could ask about evolution without being called blasphemers?

Who is the man who laughed at bourgie Negroes saying, "We don't grow collard greens out here"?

Who is the disabled vet who made the Fred Sanford dance funkier?

Who is the one-good-arm man who could wrap a gift so pretty it looked professional?

Who is the math dad who loaned me his drafting tools for making a school project but didn't make fun of my wavy lines?

Who is the man who tossed a tennis ball with the same hand he then served with?

Who is the trickster who somehow tied his laces with one loop yet shuddered at the thought of wearing loafers?

Who is the PTSD conqueror who hid a yellow arm under shirt sleeves and asked us to roll up the sleeve of his good brown arm?

Who is the napkin doodler?

Who is the divorcé keeping the family branches together?

Who is the man who never gardened, who dug up a rose-of-sharon tree with his one good hand for replanting of a bit of Cleveland home in Tuscaloosa?

THE 40 ACRES EXISTS

BUT WE WILL LIVE IN TOWN

BECAUSE YOUR MOTHER

AND YOU CHILDREN

REFUSE TO BE COUNTRY

He did it

Made it happen

That move

Embrace of yes

Lessened the grip on "no"

Grabbed day

Wheels

Propulsion

Sun and air conditioner

Early and dewy

Dark or slippery humid

Morning close

Astral ancestral

Said, "So long"

To training young white math boys

For promotion over brothers

The country called Down South

Vast vestal

Traffic behind him

65 South

Dips

Curves

Climbs

Ahead

Practiced focus

One-armed WW2 vet prowess

Reigning in day nightmares

Retaining dew

Avoiding wildlife teetering on medians

Ramping up the ultimate, the African American comeback story

Willed into now

40 acres

To hold

Wife won't live in the country   kids are city too

Dad's prerogative

No chickening out mid-challenge

Childhood friends, south to CLE migrants, advisors, family angels, Universe, God

Said, "Your teenagers are too old to move. It's a different life down there."

Yes

Him driving

Late with the dream but the dream, just the same

Daughter says

Too dark

Much too

For seeing

CLE eyes

Not quite adjusting

To subtropical

Unsure

In a recreated there

Where's East, The Lake?

Queen Anne's Lace and periwinkle

Erie

Daughter is crushed, but is always "Daddy's Girl"

Son can adapt, he thinks, "Daddy's Boy"

Daddy's "about-to-be young adults"

Pumping gas

Window washing webs of tiny flying things

Lives and psyches

Thank Buddha

Thank Malcolm X

Thank W. E. B. DuBois

Thanks woodland spirits

Jehovah

Jacob and his Ladder

Thanks trees, cardinals, crow

Wind snow

The Rapid

Lee Harvard   See you

Civil Service   See you

Mom's Shaker teacher tenure   See you

Rockefeller and your dimes   See you

University Circle   See you

Mount Pleasant   See you

West Side Market   See you

Edgewater   See you

Terminal Tower   See you

Best Location in the Nation   See you

See   you   later   Cavs   Browns

Wahoo, he never believed in you

Good-by plum and sour cherry trees

He's moving closer to peaches and pecans

A&M alumni, we'll see you at The Classic in Birmingham

To the sidewalks he organized

Bye for now

Working since 14

Gave it all to these places   *Gone*

It took a lot of Caledonia

Tons of Stardust

Loads of Mona Lisa

To get here

With a whistle and song

MOUNDVILLE

nobody leaves this heaven by the river willingly
somebodies must've smelled gun across the river

                                        black warrior

a forced retreat in all directions
north to sky to Cherokee
south to Seminole to mother earth
no robust well-nourished people
of projectile point jaws
and poison strong features
grows bored surviving

surely the mounds protect the prehistoric
from Time's gift shop motif
archaeology is a bitch
if you don't have some *yaupon holly*
some *ilex vomitoria* tea to swallow
or throw in its nosy face
the black drink purifies like fire
lives you longer than cottonwoods

                                        sycamores

is it you who eats the muscadine?
wild Alabama grapes whose leaves you hide in
hide you from trinket festivals
for school buses of pointing mean-no-harms

30 years cannot be average life span
mississippi sungods need you longer than that
from still-lifed weavers of reed
just beyond mound c

        i may find you in a bowl of arrowheads

can that be you hoodooing the kitschy kits:
dream catcher earrings dream catcher key chains
delivering nightmares to roving wannabe
                Indians

BAD BAMA HABIT

There once was a Bear. His name was Bryant. He is dead. You would not know it. Is still referred to in living tenses. Is a favorite weekend party guest. He is plaid. A houndstooth hat, a game day hologram walking through walls, showing up to snarl traffic at cocktail kickoff time. A good wager? Always. Did he abet civil rights by allowing the black ones to catch passes and do what they do—run like long-limbed hell? Was his final innovation a black quarterback who gave good interview? BEAR figured out how to beat Old Miss and Tennessee, how to make winning games a social movement. He knew those fellas COULD RUN. Bred to do it from Kill-a-Nigga, Texas to the Mason Dixon Line. They wouldn't need reading, writing, 'rithmetic for years.

Bear was GOD. Provided wins every home game. Bestowed on players the best dorms and chef made grub. Recruited this one's friend, that one's cousin who could probably run just as fast. Gave 'em scholarships and got that one's mama a car, a Buick deuce and a quarter. Who bet on the dogs, chased skirts and got religion so as to procure some Negroes for their fields? The climate rained Wins. And the rest is history. BEAR recruited one young man whose grandfather served the best chitlins since Arkansas. The least Bear could do.

I was in high school when my family moved to BEAR COUNTRY, Tuscaloosa, Alabama, where Gov. George Wallace stood in the schoolhouse door to block integration. The *schoolhouse* was actually an auditorium on U. of Alabama's antebellum campus, a few steps away from whitewashed slave cabins hiding in full view of the president's mansion. Dad retired young for a black man. Wanted to move back South, back home. Spend time with family, his aging heroes. The police tailed him, often. A black man. Retired? Must be a drug dealer.

Here's the deal. Tuscaloosa was a college town of Civil Rights vets, good ol' boys, educators and colorful club sophisticates moving uneasily in a vibrant intellectual climate edged with civic uplift and gut bucket. There is a historically Black Stillman College, the historically notorious used to be White University and several other higher learning spots. There is an "across the tracks" and a "Bottoms." There are not so humble subdivisions. And rumblings about a fraternity-sorority let's preserve whiteness alumni machine. Any day of the week, you can hear or participate in good music. Get your roots, gospel, choral or arena or indie or blues or soul or improvised on.

I've never been called out of my name there. I made friends with iconoclasts. Had a good time hanging with 2nd and 3d cousins. Still, I'm a little uneasy about my Alabama tenure. I kind of enjoy the ambivalence wave hitting me every time I hear Sweet Home . . . you know the rest. I boycott that badass riff like it's a Montgomery bus circa 1955. When Lynyrd Skynyrd sings, "In Birmingham we love the governor," as in George "Segregation Now Wallace," I can't participate.

INT.
Wood-paneled den
(daughter imitates high school cheerleaders for her parents)

DAUGHTER
If yew cain't dew
The Bear Boo-ga-loo
Just hang it up

My parents are teary with laughter. I am crying for real.

A few of my friends participated in *beauty walks*, a thing I didn't understand. I missed my Cleveland summer job, taking The Rapid downtown with friends to see plays, even riding a bike. Biking was almost nonexistent—way too hot.

Taking a city bus was rarely done. Folks drove to Birmingham or Atlanta or New Orleans for the big concerts, though there was local scene catering to townies and college types. High school kids hung out at the colleges. House parties for teens happened less than in CLE. College sports were bigger. College frat parties—huge-est. Marching band, especially on the black side of town was a euphoria-inducing sonic spectacle. By the time I joined, the funk was toned down to accommodate integration.

My African American friends, especially the girls, weren't *allowed* out much. They had those genteel cautious daddies who knew, though I didn't, that Imperial Wizard Robert Shelton was having quietly ugly KLAN meet-ups just outside of town.

A Beauty Walk is just like it sounds. No talent. No question and answer. There is just one category. You walk in your fru-fru-frock. You are judged. There's no question *the sisters* rocked their beauty at one of the first integrated ones. Not a make up wearer, I was surprised at the level of detail. I sat through a few of these until the gowns started to hoop and the sisters became mocha latte Scarlett O'Haras. The only day I giggled was when my friend's sister, a gorgeous Mexican and Navajo attitudinal diva, walked the walk celebrating her brown-ness, her curves, in a strapless sarong that can best be described as looking like something out of a Gauguin painting. I believe the reference was deliberate and I caught it, having been raised in the Cleveland Museum of Art. The confederates were gagging at her confidence. How dare she be so ethnic and dark and serious. Not smiling. Is she black? Her sister, my friend Shari was lighter of hue and allowed to pass into "K" Club. When word leaked Shari was nominating a couple of black girls for membership, some put their feet down. "*No*" I heard through the "how dare she" gossip waves.

I resigned from a community theater production of SHOWBOAT. No pickaninny fish gotta swim choreography for me. I didn't understand why an actress of color, not me but someone, was never considered for the role of the *mulatto* Julie. *Can't help hatin' dem stereotypes*. I was not about to give up my identification with Cleveland's rusty river and artist fertile gardens. No *roll-tide roll* for me. Even though I dig the poetry and potency of a poisonous tide unleashing itself on an opponent. I'm proud of never having attended a BAMA football game.

The infuriating thing about Tuscaloosa is that it's not exactly the country. It's not particularly redneck or rural. It has progressive sides and people who would be mortified to be lumped in with that vaguely confederate thing. That son of an idiot who argued that slavery wasn't *that bad*—the whole food, shelter, meaningful work argument—wasn't one of the progressives. I overheard a school administrator saying, "Civil Rights is over. Kids don't need to get stirred up reading about those times in text books."

I was already stirred up. In every city I'd lived in—Newark, DC, New York, Cleveland twice, disturbing the status quo was *the thing*. Sisters and brothers let their feelings be loudly known about unequal everything, then got down to strategizing.

"Which house should we burn out here?" a young blood knocked on the door to ask my father, when we lived in DC. "If you burn them, *the last white family on the block*, you burn us too." Dad's story. I pretend to remember.

I looked up to the Black Panthers in Jamaica, Queens, marching in formations as they guardianed the South Side with what felt like love. I was a conscious 16-year-old looking back at my 6-year-old self playing with pan-African history flash cards.

In Cleveland, I'd studied French for at least 6 years and Latin for 2. The French teacher in Tuscaloosa upon hearing of my language history told me that I would have trouble with 11th grade French because most students from West End, read the Black World, didn't take well to it. Ignorant. My folks encouraged me to take the class if I wanted. They assured me I would win. I declined.

What I needed more of was **Black Alabama Backbone**. Past registering shock and hurt, **BABB** makes a plan, trains the committed, stages an action, documents it, studies, refines it, comes back again better than new. **Black Alabama Backbone** often comes wrapped in elegant and eloquent or folksy and fun-loving packages but is as far away from a joke as you can get. They rose up. Rising. I didn't know I was going to school with the children of **BABB**. Uprisers being quiet. Watching, waiting, seeing. Not bothering to register the ones who wouldn't speak to you at the mall but would inch closer to see your homework answers. I had the fortune to meet a few of my father's former high school teachers, then retirees. I caught a glimpse of how that backbone was knitted, that quilting party of **nothing** can stop you. My new neighbors, my few new friends, out of necessity, had it. They were able to block out more of the confederate noise, I guess, from experience., a noise I had been shielded from on previous visits south.

I've got some of it now, that **BABB**. BABB has helped me navigate more than a few racial landmines as a college student in Boston.

LIVING TOO FULL IN THE PAST
MOON SITS ON HER SHOULDER
WHISPERING WHISPERS BYGONES

GIRL WHO LIVED NEXT DOOR *(ringing door bell while speaking)*
Mr. G, what's wrong with the house?

MY FORMER NEIGHBOR
Who?

GIRL WHO LIVED NEXT DOOR
It's—

MY FORMER NEIGHBOR
Who is it? *(speaking through a closed side door)*

GIRL WHO LIVED NEXT DOOR
We used to live next door—

MY FORMER NEIGHBOR
(opens the door) How are—

GIRL WHO LIVED NEXT DOOR
Fine, Mr. G. everybody's fine but I'm having bad dreams about the house.

MY FORMER NEIGHBOR
Funny you say that. Things haven't been right over there since you all moved.

GIRL WHO LIVED NEXT DOOR

What's going on?

MY FORMER NEIGHBOR

Nothing legal. (beat) How long you in town for? Where're you staying?

GIRL WHO LIVED NEXT DOOR

With Mrs. Hyche. She mentioned some things were changing.

MY FORMER NEIGHBOR *(changing the subject)*

Mrs. Hyche had that nice cherry tree. She couldn't stop the kids from coming in her yard. I couldn't stop the kids from coming in *my yard or your* yard to pick cherries from *my* tree. Before you leave here, go in the back. Pick what you want. I've got a bag you can use. Mrs. Hyche just might make you a pie like she used to.

GIRL WHO LIVED NEXT DOOR

You think I'm crazy.

MY FORMER NEIGHBOR

No, I have a question for you. Can you see to pick a good horse at Thistledown?

GIRL WHO LIVED NEXT DOOR

I'll have to look that one up. You know Dad gave me a "how to" book on E.S.P.

MY FORMER NEIGHBOR

You don't say. Well, I was just kidding. I don't gamble. My relaxation is tending impatiens.

GIRL WHO LIVED NEXT DOOR

Gorgeous flowers—those purple and white ones.

MY FORMER NEIGHBOR

What's your father growing down there? Anything?

GIRL WHO LIVED NEXT DOOR

He's working on something. Trying to get started.

MY FORMER NEIGHBOR

I used to talk to him about his hedges getting high. He handled those big clippers. Took him longer but he got it done.

GIRL WHO LIVED NEXT DOOR

With that one good arm—he had that challenge thing in him.

MY FORMER NEIGHBOR

You know it. You here for work or vacation?

GIRL WHO LIVED NEXT DOOR

I'm teaching over at Gracemount. Poetry.

MY FORMER NEIGHBOR

Poetry. You have the imagination for it.

GIRL WHO LIVED NEXT DOOR

You're making fun.

MY FORMER NEIGHBOR

No, no. I understand. I'm from Columbus, GA. This is all Georgia, Alabama, Tennessee up and down these blocks. Your father, all of us know about sight. (beat) Who I'd like to see is your brother. I remember when he was running around here jumping off the garage with my youngest.

GIRL WHO LIVED NEXT DOOR

We were a little old for that when we moved.

MY FORMER NEIGHBOR

That's a good memory. Just boys being boys. Don't tell me you used to jump off that garage roof!

OPENING THE HYMNING ROOM SINGING THE MATERNAL LINE

Find some blackberries for cobbler making
bake into dollars
stamp squeeze berry juice
jam wine hollers
shush don't tell of my
blackberry wine shine song
no one takes drinks inside these four walls
'cept my tasters

"Is it all right?"

Slurp your coffee saucer quick clean
secret to religion
to me being good at un-holy things
who can piece a quilt in minutes?
whisper biscuits   grow your hair long and baby soft?
pick more cotton than a short woman should?

Yours truly
4 foot eleven inches of
catching more fish than most men could
paying me in old clothes
will be returned to sender
pay me with that hen there
can coax any hen to lay eggs bigger

This day's got 26 eggs and hours
two more for singing time
altogether 7-year-olds and 74s
we open up the hymning room
might be in the field right before dinner time
patting juba trickstering time
leader me, my name Lee *is*
swing my arm down keep y'all in time
all day long is hymning time
is you work or song?
sing back to me bright as Sunday

Hymning rooms keep sun up longer
render work a little shorter
learn from Lee
everybody can
um, hm—even you
open up your hymning room
sing with somebody beside or besides you

That's my grandmother
one of the Wiregrass Singers at WOZK
a motley crew of babies and elders
Mr. So and So is falling asleep on his feet
Miss Wig-cocked to the side is wearing her flair
I'm tickled proud

You think it's uncool?
your grandmama's not on tv
blinging geometric shaped notes with a quirky choir
beautiful on cable access

That heritage sound—
I should've jumped in

A couple of times I went with her
to singing conventions
in that hot place where GA, FL, AL meet
geese ducks turkey ran around
slat wood buildings
I was a parched Cleveland child doing the same
I didn't know what not to do with the heat

Now I wished I had gone inside
soaked up culture

Lee complains of being last on program
knowing everyone would leave after her
sweet voiced offering
sated
"You shoulda knowed me when I had wind"

HAINT BLUE

a teenage Lomax
I listened as I drove past
his metal shingles

His first House was a job
Tuscaloosa Ice House *Coffee Boy*

Sir

COFFEE BOY ire *irie*
Barely there then
More present as current
Pensioner
Refurbishing itch
No such retiring of pine
Or bones
Bike riding
Like a kid on Christmas break

Mr.—
Indulging his silver discus quest

Cross cuts indention intention
Here in the heat where no one does that
New furniture newshine cars preferred
76 years old

Was it a space heater

Taunting you with dares
Or heirlooms begging to be saved?
Whispering furniture gone poltergeist awry

Eat fire, did you

Like La Wanda Paige's Vegas good times
Or did you freeze years ago
Catch a subtropical hard winter
Huddle up with Sanford and Son
Become a Pure Process
Stand up coffee ice cream cone
With salt pepper sprinkles?
We have yet to notice your hand-picked replacement
HubCap Man/Coffee Boy of Peanut Hill

Lotta reverends down here
Are you one?

What was your need to decorate with metal?
Pretty heat trap of snowflakes protozoa spirogyra
Endless wheels of patter
Spokes speaking
Hubcap home
Deflectors
Erector set reflectors
Interceptor of the vile eye

Reel or will in a wheel
Shine design
Obelisk a disk
Invoke a spoke
Wall of wheel
Droning door

Winding woods
Slats singing
Shekere shingles
Revolving roof

59

This house is flippant
More sassy than humble
A pretty silver landed showboat

Silvery not old

Dreaming of sea
Singing and ing-ing

Free form Poppa

Permeate this dance of a house
Come back out as Screaming Jay Hawkins
Lose your curiosity about saunas
You will come back showing how to hold shit down
Yours and the hood's

Mineral Doctor

Against some hellacious heaviness
Did you want to preserve preserves more than
inviting integration?
You used to play with white kids anyway
Your generation always says
You played together for awhile
Until
The customary
End of civility

Flow with the Bottle Tree Road
Haint Blue Hennessy Brown Everyday Green or Milk of Magnesia glass
Berries Petals Leaves protect
Those who still sweep their yards edible
Listen to dirt
Copper oxide
Glass
Haunt

CREPUSCULAR PORTRAITS

TRIO OF CROWS BEFORE CRASH, '28

"AS ONE HUNDRED AND FORTY-FIFTH STREET WAS NEARED, AN AIRPLANE CIRCLED LOW AND RELEASED A FLOCK OF BLACKBIRDS." —JAMES WELDON JOHNSON, ON THE FUNERAL CORTEGE FOR SINGER FLORENCE MILLS

Fat black warblers

       Daring dangling

                       Diagonally

Fat trapeze bird

        Beak open

                  Head up

Warbling

                  Head down   sleeping

Cawing line

       Birdhouse prop

                      Set piece

Show

        Bird up

                       Down bird

There you go

      I promote

Therefore

You

Are

Sing thing

Wing it

Like

I know you

Can

Roost

On my wrist

Our tryst is

Time

Profit time

Black bottom

Time

Hoofing time

Tan calf time

Shimmy time

Smile big time

Four four time

Cut time

1 . . . 2

1 . . . 2

My time is everything you do

                                      is every

                                                              everything

you do

                        My time is everything you do

                                    My time is everything

                                    you do

ADELAIDE'S HALL, THE FLORIDA
LONDON, 1940

NEWS REEL ANNOUNCER:

> *Grab a torch and charmer and come along. And waiting to follow is a great artist who millions have*
> *heard on the air. Here she is on the screen singing a song as only she knows how—Miss Adelaide Hall,*
> *formerly of Harlem, NY. Miss Hall and her husband Bertram Hicks are the proprietors of The Florida.*

ADELAIDE (sings a Sy Oliver tune as she hoofs)
IT'S THE PLACE THAT YOU DO IT

> > *stomp brush step*

TIME THAT YOU DO IT

> > *brush ball change*

WAY THAT YOU DO IT

> > *stomp brush step*

THAT'S WHAT GETS RESULTS

Double covered windows
bat blind air patrol
Who can see to do any damage and who doesn't love a party?
Tell the Germans to come in
I'm in the mood for some volunteer kick line
an impressionist for the War Effort
a chap who does a passable Churchill
someone who can handle her espionage cocktails

and night raid rehearsals
someone who out *shimmy shams* the *sham sham*

You
in the shiny two-piece bathing suit
A contortionist certainly stands out 'mongst the gown and tails set
My husband and I are partial to anyone who does unexpected things upside down
He's a free mind West Indian
hellion smart at business
Waits a table only
when we're short-handed
just to feel the sweep of progress
and watch faces change when he comes clean
We own The Florida

Flip, Darling, or something
Entertain, please, for the love of London
I couldn't ask that for New Rochelle
The so-called upper crust smoked us out

Crazy Love of London calms everybody
especially if we rev them uptown style first
I'm talking Harlem where we flip while we jazz
and Brooklyn where the band scrambles you eggs in the dark
I've been hoofing with closed eyes since bringing Art Tatum from Cleveland . . . or was it Toledo?
I put him on you know for my New York show
He was from out there, was regaling the boonies
playing a sound in Cleveland like two player-pianos at once
Tatum played all the clubs around 105th   music streets and afterhours
left hand and right striding ragging jazzing outdoing each other
I told him, "I can get you much more than beer tips for your blind tricks."
I was talking New York money apples dropping in his lap for those skills
Tatum could bite big with what he could do

La Grosse Pomme-our littlebig nightclub in Paris
showcased hot talent for flushed temperaments
Some nerve we have being colored in Europe

Miss *What's-your-name*
I can recall a song title
North American bird species and their whistles
dance steps
names I want to forget
trials   trifles   *stomp brush step brush ball change*
Let me see you try

COMPASS

NO MAP

CORPOREAL

MIGRATION

SYMPATHETIC MAGIC

No pictures, no video. Please honor my quest to be unremembered, unfixed in time, unreflected, un-captured through a pinhole, lasered, over/under-exposed, covered in shadow, birthed on shiny paper, worse yet in cyberspace, a wholesoul, un-inclined to leave the body in snaps and shots, in flashes. I am allergic to digital damage, fragmentation, removal of parts and selves, leaving the body by iPhone.

Feel me now this place where we can eyeball us/become the lowest down blues, sanctified bolero, bata drums, massage you from your tree roots sucking your soca toes, kneading calves, hammering Congolese knees, urging your hips to intelligence, shaking, swaying to "in between the beats" with everything you got to shimmy with. No anorexic groove here, this is voluptuous funktified pathos, an emotional transmuting samba.

This small room is our soul. Right Now. Shared oxygen, sweat, enough salt and smack talk spice up the margaritas. You bite your nails. I ouch. You savor liquor, conversation, ice. I relax. I know the conversation's gist, thought my name in Bennet and I'm soooo not in it. The stage is you. I am on. You are curtain. Your teeth are lights. Specials. I feel my light in your laugh. Glasses off, I know you by your outline, your heart. No need to see features. I feel your heart with me in this performed journey.

I'm a soul thief, caught pilfering my own anima. An enslaved to gaps, too shy to be fine, wigged out perfectionist meets image control freak goes cuckoo. Crazed after a wedding or party or reunion or chance get together with friends at the pier, I call everybody, "Please do not post my picture on social media. Please do not post my picture on social media. Please do not post my picture on social media. And do not put me in your kitchen in a digital picture frame. Do not have me blinking with the stove timer. Mirror crash. Obscurity wish— to be un-remembered.

TWISTED CAROLS

1.Joni Cary was either a Muslim or a Jehovah's Witness. At 6 years old, I confused religion and denomination. Both didn't celebrate Christmas or say the pledge of allegiance at school. In her UpSouth flavored *all-about–the-Bah Humbug*, Joni would drawl, "Ain't no Santa Claus," running me home in tears. Despite all, I wasn't even close to giving up Brother Claus to the ghost of Kill Joy Present. He slid down our non-working chimney into the fireplace. Drank the hot chocolate we made. I eyeballed him—a cheerful, middle-aged, copper brown man with a salt and pepper beard and silky mini fro. He ate the Easy Bake sugar cookies, too.

Dad hadn't yet started to say after checking our lists one and a half times and with some anxiety altering his super cool, "We give Santa the money for your toys."

(Sung to the tune of Silent Night) *Santa ain't going broke. Santa ain't going broke. Some call it middle class and that's no joke. Yes, it matters our college degrees. Your mother is getting her Ph.D. We're rich in education. Don't you love getting books under the tree?*

2.The Jackson Five's "I Saw Mommy Kissing Santa Claus" was the most embarrassing song ever. You know how Michael used to do it. High-voiced, beautiful, poignant. Forgive me for trying: *If Daddy had only seen Mommy kissing Santa Claus last night.* Maybe I was starting to understand the real deal. At that time, kind of like now, I had a real make believe friendship with little Michael Jackson which means Mommy was kissing Papa Joseph Jackson which is slightly frightening. What embarrassed me more was Dad hating fake trees but determined not to overspend on real ones. All season, I had to hear cracks about our Charlie Brown Christmas tree. No one had an original joke—just the Charlie Brown thing. All I wanted for Christmas was a big beautiful evergreen like the one at Higbee's, once one of Cleveland's big old Miracle on 34th St. looking department stores where I used to stand in the Santa Claus line looking a bit overgrown and pre-teen although I was pre-tween and hanging on to kid-dom as long as I could.

3. **Washington**, **DC**, home for a minute, fomented my fear of The Nutcracker—the character, not the kitchen tool, and all manifestations thereof. Beautiful music for scary teeth dolls, Dangerous Dancing Humans dressed as bigger than limb-cracking life statues. Kind of like when after visiting George Washington's home, Mount Vernon, I started having nightmares about the paintings there—portraits of colonials with powdered white faces and whitened wigs. Not understanding pallor fashion, I'd wake up screaming, "Mommy, Mommy—the white people!" One of my mother's teacher colleagues gifted her a huge and beautiful homemade gingerbread man. Mom brought it home, excited to show my brother and me. I took one look at the thing and was inconsolable. I didn't understand the consumption of friends, let alone covering them with icing and spices. Perhaps that's why I became plant-based.

5. *Joy to the world the Cuisinart has come. Let Earth receive her recipes. Let every stomach prepare her room*. Mom is smart. She uses big words. I have to ask her to slow down sometimes so I can keep up. If I say, "Mommy, I love you." She might say something like, "It's reciprocated, Dear." Mom cooks ideas, not cookbooks or cooking or even food at times. She often skimps on the salt, and definitely on the portions. For Mom, Nutrition is a synonym for portals accessed through the World of Word, a Toni Morrison turn of syllable. The rarest air of her book collection is a tribute to Black and Art and Movement.

6. Mom cooks soul food from recipes, yet drives herself *crazy* trying to reproduce my grandmother's *gravy*, her southeastern Alabama cuisine. Grandma never used recipes. Dad scared two of his kids into being vegetarians by talking about what happens to the colon. "Meat just sits there, Sweetie, and festers." Mom now fusses over her vegetarian Christmas recipes much as she did the colon-festering ones—anything to make an almost seasonal depressive like me happy. And I'm grateful.

GAME DAY RETREAT OR 40 ACHES

Acre 40

Sell?   not growing a thing

no collards   turnips   wild onion, maybe

rabbit grass grow   I call the wife
                              ask timber or hunting permission

no land making money neither

            He, the husband, rest in peace   maimed from the war
                                        couldn't stand a gun's company

VietnamKorea?   Mighta been before

Hated guns so much their new years was always shotless quiet

wishes to the Big Dipper

Acre 39, too?   blooming taxes

                                   Scrub grass & pines

                                   No goodluck collards
                                     trusty turnips

The daughter'd know what to do with Acre 38

have her big white tent dress up graduation party

vibrating and strobing monster light to beats to early light

from Central, Kennedy, Marshall, Shaker, Laurel, US, HB, Hawken, Beaumont, Heights, Warrensville

schoolmates meeting up like social media, the **O-H-I-O**

materializing into Alabama roots even if their people was from Virginia, Texas, the Carolinas

what's an American without a stutter step squawk?

without a drag your foot drawl?

without stanky leg talk?

without shout enunciation?

without second line intonation?

accents changeable as wind

That daughter with her Cleveland talk sounds more downhome than the parents

These black upnorths need to know wherefrom they got their backbones

Acre 37

They gon' build a house on it

They not gon' build on it

It's just sittin' here while they live in town

The wife teaches at the college

Why would she live over here?

That girl is going back UpNorth

They was from Cleveland

I was up there when that daughter was a little tyke

When somebody brown got paid to burn our neighborhoods down

Daughter carries a torch for a Cleveland ain't there no more

What do I know about the New Cleveland?

I know those Negroes got to going to the white dry cleaners and doctors soon as one door

Opened and an overpass cut the hood in two

Just like down here

Watch out when they start getting good at doing our hair

They're teaching that, I hear, in beauty-barber school

Acre 36

You either know about subsurface rights

Hardwood creek bottoms pine plantations

Let the land make you some green

Hunting parties or game day cabins

That daughter would have this being a safe house for the past

You can't hide Martin Luther King or Autherine Lucy or

Vivian Malone or James Hood anymore than you could

Kidnap The Bear if you got sick of him

Or Woodie Hayes if you wanted to be entertained

By a coach for a change instead of players

I know the daughter the son the wife the husband have love for Stillman's Tigers

But never a Crimson Tide

The wife's mother liked to fish

The husband's grandfather knew what all the plants of the forest healed

The girl shoulda learned about subsurface in them Cleveland schools

This land pie is a slice of minerals, pines and air

Is what they pay taxes on worth keeping?

Canoeing on the Sipsey (a consideration of water)

That daughter would be friends with sandshell mussel

A sunfish

A cypress tree

Canoe this backwater congeal

Holler at pine trees

Before claiming kinship

With The Tide

She wants them running backs

To read good

Good as they can run

That daughter

Saw Steel Pulse at Foster's Auditorium

The notorious schoolhouse door

Full of maroons roots raising the roof

No Crimson nowhere but dreams of Burning Spear

Black post colonial Rastafari face

No Scarlett hoop skirts

Crowns and stoles of natty dreads singing:

That's why I and I nah sit down inna no back bench

Natty like to be bright, bright, bright

Out here too dark for stars

for sight

for driving

almost to Mississippi

stopping to mark it

Ready or not

She

is there

here

BROWN'S CIRCLE

They could have moved into the Brown's Circle house
The house that married them in dresses hats suits in the 50s
A few friends from Stillman witnessed
Batiste's Baton Rouge-y gumbo for the reception
Whiskey drinkers clinking glasses with the ginger ale set
Men back from the war stuffing their worldliness into college desks
College girls picturing the New York life or a requisite move somewhere

Don't listen to the kids
Forget the basement
See that barbecue pit
that land back there
Add on to the house
Modern it up
More room than a Cleveland bungalow
You tell the kids
You're moving them here
Don't go soft now
Tell them the rental income paid their private school tuition
Seen and humored
Indulge too much they'll need you too much when you're old enough to need them
Whatchu say Brown's Circle?
You were hoping for run around on the grass babies
House, I hate to break it to you
These babies are about to go to college
There will be no grass trampling fun in this heat

H & L EXPRESS: A BARBER/
BEAUTY ESTABLISHMENT

FOR REVEREND LINTON AND THE STUDENTS

I'm a shaving mug collecting Papa
If you want to see me hurry
all you gotta do is tell me about a swap meet

I'm a plainspoken confidently humble servant of God and no man
Mr. and Mizz
I'm a monster of preservation
You want to see a Civil Rights Cherish Doll for all seasons
A Nationally treasured yet slightly unknown member of your family?
Look about   at the pictures   all around the shop

Let them be the Super Heroes they already are
Point to a photograph I'll tell you who worked out the strategy
who cleaned up the coeds on that side   the women's sink
students trying to integrate college while eggs and garbage and I don't know what all
were being thrown at them
We shaved off all their hair if they were tear-gassed
comforted everyone who came through
hid a few from the authorities
treated injuries while the boycott was happening in T-Town's downtown
the hospital, we refused to go to
Called in our own doctors to treat these children

They come back and see us

if they haven't blocked the experience

being smoked out of your education

tear-gassed on First African Baptist ground

Was there a Selma strategy without Tuscaloosa?

Without a young minister, T. Y. Rogers recommended by Martin King

and the times?

We hated doing it—shaving the naïve off young people

Girls and boys

Had to arm them somehow with something durable

A durable sheen

This shop was a safe house

We showed what to do in a non-violent situation

Gone the other way

Hear shots?

Everybody drops to the ground

Man throws his whole self over the woman

Covers the child

If any head looks up

It's his

BARRETTES AND GINGER SNAPS

All girls
All girls
So many all girls
5 Black girls
Nice Asian girl
White wavy girls
Jewish curly girls
Confusing hair girls
Jet Italian girl curls
Crimped or curled Black girl perms
Almost straightening combs and Afros

Here I am in a private school uniform with variations
Hemlines sanctioned and not:
Blue green plaid skirt yellow button down
Green wool skirt yellow button down or baby blue
Green white herringbone skirt yellow or baby or dark blue button down
Short sleeved Izods
Cardigans
Pullovers

5 of us homegirls splash painted color on a rare world 7th grade
Rode The Rapid way out from urban edges
To giant art studios and field hockey green

My Black public school was rare world too
Boo koos of subjects

Small but major "gifted" classes

Nous parlons français

Smart Black and tracked

Rad teachers and Blackfolk love at our backs

Mom was never crazy about cherry picked progressive education

For a few

But there I was

Having un-thrived in "regular" class

Paddled with holey splintery wood and indignation

Better to break down a girlchild jumping up for her accuracy

Lexiconed levels

A progressive leaving

Regular Enrichment Major Work

Word on the pre-teenybopper street

Some were moving to *Super Duper Major Work*

Major Work then Super Duper turned out to be a moving on up in another school

Gracemount School

The *you'd better thoroughly research your Daily Talk* school

The *we expect elocution excellence* school

The *get your acting improvisation on and singing in French* school

My 4th grade debate with Sandra before the entire student body:

Armed resistance vs. Non-violent direct action

Our babytake on Black and Power

I was more into painting designs on the wide windows of the car store with Jennifer and the art talented who tolerated me

Or arranging a "Ben" a la Michael Jackson duet to sing with Fawn at the next school concert

Co-choreographing with Lori to the Ohio Players for student government elections

Or Re-writing lines of the class play

Making a costume I didn't have the eye or patience to bring to life

Swimming in my East side gifted public school pool
Gave me gumption and a few high stakes stomachaches
The semester I grazed a chess tournament's bottom

You didn't bring home anything but EXCELLENT grades!
Socially you got points being pretty fine handsome
As cute as a Jackson or a Sylver
Michael and Jermaine or Janet   Ricky or Foster or Charmaine
Hair at least shoulder length or big 'fro voluminous
EXCELLENT grades!

You had to sing, dance, hand dance, play, act—*something*
At house parties you dance cool-eclectically not stepping on toes or making
concentrating-too-much faces

Your clothes had to be cute but not just on performance days
If you could run dance and look cute at all times you were good

You're Black so you were born chasing wind on asphalt, slide
stepping on ice, kicking dodging batting catching running your Heisman trophy run
jumping like Olympians even if not particularly sportive

Did Woody Hayes want you to skip junior high to enroll at Ohio State?

Barely layered up in the cold
We never wore sneakers—it was tennis shoes

THE JEALOUSY I TRY TO FORGET

Mr. Kowalski asked Karamu actress and fellow teacher Carol Banks to direct his class his regular class in
To Be Young Gifted and Black

Nobody in Major Work or Super Duper Major Work was involved except as alternately thrilled and sullen
audience

Carol Banks in her leotard and flowing skirt—
Boss Afro'd Carol Banks of long and eloquent arms was married to actor
Ron "Super Fly" O'Neal

The children *SANG*

The *stretch and arch of our too lucky dancing schoolmates*

BY 7TH GRADE TIME

We public school kids were ready for the academic rigeurs of prep—
anybody's private school

Plus rolling, bouncing, skating, playing touch football on a schoolyard ice slick
educates your balance
You're never too cool to fall

Being in class with a Black math genius named Erica
shows you possibilities

Great as the public was I wanted the private

We were Midwest preppers with an East coast outlook

I wanted that rugby-flavored lemonade

That ivy draped Harvard look

This exo-urban new-to-me school where the Major Work kids went

And would branch out from to build on Black

I lived too close to the city's edge to become a suburban demographic

Not that there weren't Black folks living deep into the east side suburbs

Because there were and tenaciously so

But I was still a city kid

All the cool I tried too hard to radiate

Nullified by a field trip in a uniform to the Orchestra

In the middle of public school freely expressed wardrobes

I was beyond glad to be around boys

But was someone actually raining paper clips down on us during tuning?

A typical day at prep school included a mid-morning break

Us Blackgirls brought records to play

Bootsy's Rubberband and P-Funk to dance to

Between the downing of Ginger Snaps and milk

living the soundtrack's quarter tones

the fingersnap to a sound track

Grooving to the microscopic inside

Not the only thing

But part of our quotidian from way back

ONCE AND FUTURE LEBRON

Mom interviewed Muhammad Ali
who was always in CLE
turf since the 40s of Don, King Of Numbers
or in Ashtabula County
King's boxing training champion digs in the country
Ali existed in rumors of playground disruption
play sparring with school kids
showing up deadpan to clock a principal
a surprise neighborhood booster reaching behind his back
from Louisville to Kinshasa to here

Mom wasn't thinking about taking us kids with her
though John and I begged r&b poignantly
our falsetto *pleases* shut out by, "You have to go to school"
We kinda knew she didn't have time to pick us up on her lunch break
and meet The Greatest

After school was a litany of
"What was he like? How was it?
Proper Mom purred, "He is one fine looking man"
Our shock was louder than questions
We have the pictures—all of them
Mom, English teacher fine
Dad and Mr. Hyche in their best *let's get stuff done in the community* fine-ness

Ali understands hope resuscitation

like James Brown and Gorgeous George bursting through capes laid over feigned or real exhaustion bursting back to dancing, to The Show, The People

Another King, James of Akron, understands defibrillation of hope and cities

When news broke of LeBron leaving the Cavaliers for The Heat, video footage showed a few, maybe more than a few distraught fans burning any number 23 on a textile

A friend offered, "Black folks won't bother burning jerseys. They'll just let the brother go."

I know a few folks who fired up LeBron jerseys in backyard barbecue grills, sisters and brothers who wouldn't risk being arrested but found a way to effigy their profound questions

Why leave Cleveland? It's home.

ACKNOWLEDGMENTS

"Moundville" was published in *Callaloo*, Volume 20, Number 3, June 1997.

Thank you to Keith Tuma, Amy Toland, Jeff Clark and everyone at Miami University Press for cheerleading for this book.

Love to my family, family of friends and all whose affirmation convinced me that Now is the Time!

To John Lowe, Robert Jones, Tranita Benton, Lee Ann Brown, Gene Alexander Peters, Lillie Hyche-Cochran, Dark Room Collective alumni, Heroes Are Gang Leaders, Modern-Day Griot, Thomas Sayers Ellis, Artress Bethany White, John Keene, Sharan Strange, Major Jackson, Randall Horton, Charles E. Drew, Jr., Margie Duffield, Stephanie L. Jones, Suzanne Y. Jones, Nils Olaf Dolven, Nehassaiu deGannes, Jenni Lamb, James Brandon Lewis, Ronette and Team Alexis, Janice Hogan, Patricia Spears Jones, Tyehimba Jess, Melanie Maria Goodreaux, Da Frontline, Meredith Wright, Yohann Potico, Howard Alper, Eric Perl, Jared Hassan Foles, Jordan Dann, Diana Yanez, Erica Hunt, Liza Jessie Peterson, Saretta Morgan, Reverend Linton, Let it Bee Salon, Julie Patton, Arcey Hartan, Paul Van Curen, Rachel Sheinkin, Tonya Foster, Shelagh Patterson, Fred Moten, and to the editors at Belladonna Collaborative, Teachers & Writers Collaborative, and *Callaloo*, I am warmly grateful.

To Ntozake Shange, thank you for your word dance and for the layers of story in your syllable conjuring.

To Nina Simone and Gil Scott-Heron, you were and are two of the reasons.

To Mom's bookshelves, where I first encountered Amiri Baraka, Bob Kaufman, Lawrence Ferlinghetti, Paule Marshall, Kenneth Patchen, James Baldwin, Mari Evans, Toni Morrison and so many more—you were the best starter kit.

To Gladys King and Virgie Ezelle Patton, thank you for our art walks and Karamu jaunts.

JANICE A. LOWE is a poet and composer of musical theater and opera. She is the author of the chapbook *SWAM*, a short play. She performs with the experimental poetry and music group **Heroes Are Gang Leaders** and has performed with the bands **Digital Diaspora** and **w/o a net**. She composed the opera *Dusky Alice* and wrote the libretto for the song cycle *Little Girl Loose*, a collaboration with composer Nils Olaf Dolven. Her original full-length musicals, performed in New York City and regionally, include *Somewhere in Texas* (book and lyrics by Charles E. Drew, Jr.), *Lil Budda* (text by Stephanie L. Jones), and *Sit-In at the Five & Dime* (words by Marjorie Duffield). *Lil Budda* was presented at The Eugene O'Neil Musical Theater Conference and in National Alliance for Musical Theater's Festival of New Works.

Janice has composed music for the plays *Born of Conviction* by Kathryn Dickinson, *12th and Clairmont* by Jenni Lamb, *Door of No Return* by Nehassaiu deGannes, and *Shafrika, the White Girl* by Anika Larson.

Her poems appear in journals including *Callaloo, The Hat, American Poetry Review* and in the anthology *In the Tradition*. Her essays on mentoring creative writing appear in *Sing the Sun Up, From Medusa to Sky* and *Old Faithful: 18 Writers Present Their Favorite Writing Assignments*, Teachers & Writers Press.

Janice has taught Poetry and Performance at Purchase College and youth creative writing workshops in New York City.

She holds an MFA in Musical Theater Writing, New York University–Tisch School of the Arts.

She is a co-founder of the **Dark Room Collective**.

Her website is www.janicelowe.com.